CATS

First published in Great Britain 1984 by
Webb and Bower (Publishers) Limited
9 Colleton Crescent, Exeter, Devon EX2 4BY

Edited, designed and illustrated by
the E.T. Archive Limited
Chelsea Wharf, 15 Lots Road, London SW10 0QH

Designed by Julian Holland
Picture Research by Anne-Marie Ehrlich
Special photography by Eileen Tweedy
Copyright © text and illustrations E.T. Archive Ltd 1984

British Library Cataloguing in Publication Data

Loxton, Howard
    Cats.—(A Webb & Bower miniature)
    1. Cat breeds—Pictorial works
    I. Title
    636.8'7   SF447.5

    ISBN 0 86350 012 9

Phototypeset by Text Filmsetters Limited, Orpington, Kent
Printed and bound in Hong Kong by Mandarin Offset International Limited

CATS

Howard Loxton

Webb&Bower

EXETER, ENGLAND

Goddess of Bubastis

Snakes and cats were among the many animals linked with the gods and goddesses of ancient Egypt. In one manifestation the sun god Ra took cat form to conquer daily the serpent Apep, representing darkness. Paintings show him as a cat, brandishing a knife and cutting off the head of Apep.

Several goddesses were thought of in cat form or as cat-headed. The most venerated throughout Egypt was Bast, whose main cult centre was at Bubastis on the lower Nile. Here, in the courtyard of a great temple, lived sacred cats which were carefully watched by priests for any message from the goddess which their behaviour might reveal.

Thousands of devotees sailed down the Nile each year in gaily decorated boats to attend the annual cult festival at Bubastis, their music and laughter echoing across the water. Bast was a fertility goddess and the orgiastic celebrations, which survived until suppressed by the Byzantine Emperor Theodosius in AD 392, shocked visitors from other lands. However, anyone who has owned a female cat can understand the link between feline fecundity and the demands of a calling cat.

Thousands of cats were buried in catacombs at Bubastis, carefully mummified and sometimes placed in beautiful bronze coffins, so that they too should cross to the afterlife, a sign of the owners' affection for them. They viewed their cats with humour as well, depicting them in satirical situations like this cat driving geese in a procession of other animals.

Egyptian Pets

The Egyptians not only venerated cats with their gods, but they were also the first to domesticate them. The grain produced in the fertile Nile valley was the source of Egypt's wealth and the granaries attracted rodents and these in turn attracted cats, which were no doubt encouraged because they kept rodents down.

Wall paintings in numerous tombs show cats, like this one painted in the reign of Ramesses II (1292–1225 BC). The cat is wearing a collar so it is certainly domesticated and it gnaws its bone under the chair of Mutemuia who is watching her husband, Kenro, play a kind of board game. Other paintings show cats with wildfowlers in the marshes and reedbeds of the delta which were probably trained as retrievers to bring back birds knocked down by sticks.

The earliest paintings date from the sixteenth century BC but we cannot be sure which of these animals are wild cats and which are the truly domesticated type – for the domestic cat developed from the wild cats of Egypt. They were, however, regarded with great affection. Killing or deliberately harming a cat was a serious crime and the Greek historian Herodotus describes how, when a household cat died, the whole family went into mourning.

There is a legend that when, during an invasion in about 500 BC, a Persian army advanced upon an Egyptian city, the inhabitants put up no resistance because each Persian soldier carried a cat in front of him and an attack upon the soldiers would have meant injuring the cats.

7

Classical Cats

The export of domestic cats from ancient Egypt was prohibited by law but that did not prevent some of them reaching other countries, smuggled out, perhaps, by Phoenician traders. The Greeks showed little enthusiasm for them, although one does appear on its master's funeral stele and must have been a well-loved pet. Others are depicted on coins, vases from the Greek colonies and a carved statue plinth. The Greeks had a lovely name for the cat, *ailouros*, the animal with a tail which waves, though they also called it *gali*, a word which can mean a kind of weasel or polecat.

The Romans probably adopted the cat along with other exotic Egyptian cults, such as the worship of the goddess Isis, but they seem to have taken some time to appreciate its value in rodent control. There is no mention of its skills until the fourth century AD, when the agriculturalist Palladius recommended cats to protect gardens from mice and moles. Nevertheless, by then, cats had been introduced as domestic animals into Britain and other outlying parts of the Roman Empire.

The Romans linked the Egyptian cat goddess Bast with their own moon goddess Diana, and transferred the association with the cat to her and thence to Hecate, Queen of witches and closely identified with Diana. The identification with paganism and the involvement of sacrificial cats in Gallic and other fertility rites may have influenced the early Christian church against the cat, which the Roman church linked with the Devil.

A Medieval View

Mouser she is called, because she is fatal to mice. The common people call her Catus because she can catch things. Others say that it is because she lies in wait (*captat*, she watches). The glare of her eye is so acute that it penetrates the darkness with a gleam of light.

The authors of bestiaries were rarely original, but Bartholomeus Anglicus, writing in about 1260, made his own observations in *De Proprietatibus Rerum*.

He is a full lecherous beast in youth, swift, pliant and merry, and leapeth and riseth (pounces) on everything that is before him: and is lead by a straw and playeth therewith: and is a right heavy beast in age and full sleepy, and lieth in wait for mice: and is aware where they be more by smell than by sight, and hunteth and riseth on them in privy places: and when he taketh a mouse he playeth therewith and eateth him after the play. In time of love is hard fighting for wives, and one scratcheth and rendeth the other grievously with biting and with claws. And he maketh a rueful noise and ghastful, when one proffereth to fight with another: and unneth is hurt when he is thrown down off an high place. And when he hath a fair skin, he is as it were proud thereof, and goeth fast about: and when his skin is burnt, then he bideth at home, and is oft for his fair skin taken of the skinner and slain and flayed.

dilz scalpens & effodiens sibi ipsi conformat. Quidã ũ ex huis nature impio seruire parati: terrã ab aliis fossam. uentriqz supmo imposita quatuor pedibz cõplecterenes. lignoqz in ore transuerso locato: denuibz ab aliis hunc inde coherentbz retro gradeqz trahentbz: ñ absqz intuentium admiratione trahũt.

Musio appellatus [Musio] quod muribz in festui sit. hunc uulgus catum a captura uocant. Alii dicunt qd captat idest uidet. Hã tam ãtum cernit ut fulgore luminis nochis te nebras supet. Vnde a greco uenit catus idest in genosus. apotoykã Geszuz. [Mus]

Mus pusillum animal greaĩ illi nomen est quiaqd uero ex eo tra hit: latinũ sit. Alii dicunt mu rel quod ex humore tre nascantur. Nam mus tra. unde & humus. Hiis implenitu nio tetur crescit. sicut quedã maritima augentur: que rursus minuente luna deficiunt. Sorex latinũ est eo qd rodat & in modum serre precidat. Antiqui aute sorice sauricem dicebant. sicut & dodiu claudiu. Mistice aut mures significant hoies cupiditate trena intrantes. & preda

Angora Cats

The long fur of domestic cats does not occur in wild members of the cat family. The snow leopard and the northern lynx, which live in colder climes, have denser, rather than longer coats, and a thick undercoat to keep them warm. Long hair seems to be a mutation which has only been able to persist in domestic cats. The luxuriant silky hair which breeders have achieved would be difficult for any cat to keep in good condition on its own and these cats need regular brushing, at least once or twice each day.

There are said to have been no long-haired cats in Europe until the end of the sixteenth century when one was taken to France from Turkey. Longhairs became known as Angoras, for they were thought to originate in Angora, now called Ankara, in Turkey. Towards the end of the nineteenth century the heavier, round-headed Persian cat became the most popular longhair and Angoras became very rare but the breed has been revived through a special breeding programme at Ankara zoo.

> All your wondrous wealth of hair,
> Dark and fair,
> Silken-shaggy, soft and bright
> As the clouds and beams of night,
> Pays my reverent hand's caress
> Back with friendlier gentleness.
> *Algernon Swinburne, To a cat*

Cat familiars

I shall goe intill ane catt
With sorrow, and sych, and a blak shott,
And I shall goe in the Divellis nam,
Ay guhill I com hom againe.

That, according to Ysobel Gowdie, accused of witchcraft in
Scotland in 1662, was the spell by which she could turn
herself into a cat, an ability attributed to many witches.
Sometimes they were also credited with a supernatural servant, a minor devil, who made certain they did not slip out
of the Devil's power. In Britain this servant was often
thought to take the form of an animal or 'familiar'. Frogs,
toads, rabbits, lambs, dogs, moles and other animals as well
as cats were named to accuse a suspected witch. Eight-year-
old Thomas Rabbet, giving evidence against his mother in
Essex in 1582, described four familiars, 'Titty is like a little
grey cat, Tiffin is like a white lamb, Piggin is black, like a
toad, and Jack is black, like a cat'. He claimed his mother
gave them beer, white bread or cake and that at night the
spirits 'will come... and suck blood of her upon her arms
and other places of her body'.

In a savage spate of witch-hunting in 1645-6 the self-
styled 'Witch Finder General of England', Matthew Hop-
kins, sent more than two hundred suspected witches to their
deaths. Every old woman with a wrinkled face and a pet by
her side was in danger of being so accused.

The Worth of a Cat

Despite the antagonism of the Christian Church, which saw the cat as a representative of the Devil, the worth of the cat as a rodent controller was amply acknowledged and codified by law in places where Rome could be ignored. The eleventh item of the tenth-century Vendotian Code from north Wales recorded:

> The worth of a kitten, from the night it is kittened until it shall open its eyes, is a legal penny.
> And from the time that it shall kill mice, twopence.
> And after it shall kill mice, four legal pence; and so it always remains.
> Her teithi are to see, to hear, to kill mice, to have her claws entire, to rear and not devour her kittens; and if she be bought and be deficient in any one of these tiethi, let one third of her worth be returned.

In south-east Wales the Gwentian Code required that:

> Whoever shall kill a cat that guards a house and a barn of the King, or shall take it stealthily, it is to be held with its head to the ground and its tail up, the ground being swept, and then clean wheat is to be poured about it until the tip of its tail be hidden; and that is its worth.

Another contemporary code provides that if grain is not available the recompense shall be a milch sheep and her lamb and her wool, and both codes demand that a cat 'be not caterwauling on every new moon'.

17

The Tabby Cat

The European Wild Cat, *Felis sylvestris*, has tabby markings as do many examples of the African Wild Cat, *Felis lybica*, while others with spotted or agouti (brindled) fur are variations of the tabby stripe. The Wild Cat's vertical tiger stripes, from the backbone to the belly, are only one of the patterns recognized by cat-show judges and clubs as a tabby (they call it the mackerel pattern). The other, which they call the 'standard' or blotched tabby, is a more horizontal pattern with three stripes down the spine and an oyster-shaped whorl on the flanks.

In England the tabby used to be known as the Cyprus cat, suggesting an origin in the eastern Mediterranean, or somewhere beyond, with Cyprus as a staging-post on its way to Britain. Its pattern is similar to that of watered silk, or taffeta, which is not surprising for both words, taffeta and tabby are said to be derived from Attibiya, the name of a district in Baghdad famous for producing that kind of silk.

Both kinds of tabby have rings around the tail, bars on the legs, chains across the chest and delicately pencilled markings on the face and forehead, but the 'standard' tabby seems to have no parallel among wild cats and it is thought to be a mutation from the striped. By the middle of the seventeenth century it was already common in Europe, where it is now seen more frequently than the tiger stripe, but it is still a minority in India and the East.

Black Devils

In Britain, black cats are thought to bring good luck but elsewhere they are often thought unlucky. When Pope Clement V suppressed the Knights Templar at the beginning of the fourteenth century, some of its members confessed under torture that they had worshipped the Devil in the form of a black tom-cat.

In 1344, a knight arriving in Metz, where there was an outbreak of St Vitus' Dance, claimed that as he was about to sleep he saw a huge black cat sitting staring at him. He made the sign of the cross and drew his sword and the cat vanished, hissing blasphemies. Next day the victims were cured and for years thereafter cats were burned in the city square as a warning to the Devil.

Robert Downer told the court trying Susanna Martin during the Salem witch trials of 1692 that some years before he had accused her of being a witch. 'Whereat she being dissatisfied said, That some she-Devil would shortly fetch him away... The night following as he lay in his bed, there came in at the Window, the likeness of a Cat, which flew upon him, took fast hold of his Throat, lay on him a considerable while, and almost killed him. At length he remembered what Susanna Martin had threatened... and with much sriving he cried out, "Avoid, thou She-Devil. In the name of the Father, the Son, and the Holy Ghost, Avoid!" Whereupon it left him, leaped on the Floor, and flew out at the Window.'

The Necessary Cat

A home without a cat, and a well-fed, well-petted and properly revered cat, may be a perfect home, *perhaps*, but how can it prove its title?

Mark Twain, c.1890

A fine pedigreed animal or a rescued alley-cat, it does not matter what colour or type – a cat does seem to make a home complete, and the image of a cat curled up on the hearthrug before a glowing fire is the very picture of domesticity.

William Shakespeare was probably thinking of the household mouser when he wrote of the 'harmless, necessary cat', but the cat makes an affectionate and comforting companion and a lively playfellow as any caring cat owner knows and generations of cat lovers have attested. The calm of a contented cat has a relaxing effect upon the troubled mind.

Joseph Green, an eighteenth-century poet had a cat which even helped him write his verses when other inspiration failed him:

Whene'er I felt my towering fancy fail,
I stroked her head, her ears, her tail,
And, as I stroked, improved my dying song
From the sweet notes of her melodius tongue.
Her purrs and mews so evenly kept time,
She purred in metre and she mewed in rhyme.

23

Cat Thief

Cats are opportunists and rarely miss a chance to grab an extra titbit. Though they may whine and wheedle for attention, they seem to enjoy something they have stolen more than anything else. Food offered in their own dish may be ostentatiously ignored, but a cut from the very same piece of meat left on an unattended plate will become irresistibly desirable and will disappear the instant your back is turned. The thief cat displays the stealth, patience and quicksilver action which are the skills not only of the thief but of the hunter and they have been perfected by long practice.

In this Japanese woodblock print, made about 1845 by the artist Kuniyoshi, the cat has been caught stealing a fish and is being punished but, at the same time, in the upper picture his skill is being compared with that of the samurai archer hunting by torchlight in the snow.

Kuniyoshi himself was a great lover of cats and depicted them in everyday domestic scenes, in caricatures and in scenes from Kabuki plays based on the many Japanese legends which feature cats. He painted a number of self-portraits, all of which feature cats, although the artist only shows himself as seen from the back.

25

Legends of the Siamese

Early forms of the Siamese breed often had crossed eyes and a kink in the tail – now considered faults by breeders, but they were so characteristic of the breed that various rather 'Kiplingesque' stories, which might have bases more in fiction than in fact, have been offered in explanation.

One story tells of an eastern princess, who whenever she went bathing with her attendants, used to remove the rings from her fingers and place them upon the tail of her favourite cat. To make sure they were safe and would not fall off, she tied a knot in the cat's tail which has remained as a permanent kink in all Siamese cats since.

In another version, a cat was given a beautiful jewelled goblet to guard, and fearful of falling alseep and failing in its duty, it coiled its tail tightly round the stem while never taking its eyes from it. The twist left in the tail and the inward-looking eyes record the cat's devotion for posterity.

Fanciful though these stories are, they do reflect the loyalty and attachment that the Siamese cat usually shows to his owner. Conversely, they are also cats that demand a great deal of attention, taking an interest in human activities and expecting to be involved in them whenever possible.

Puss-in-Boots

Peasants in the south of France at one time widely believed that there were magician cats, known as *matagots*, who could bring prosperity to a house where they were cherished and well looked after. Naturally, these *matagots* found their way into legend and into fairy tale. The most famous of them is probably Puss-in-Boots, a cunning talking cat whose story was already popular in the Middle Ages and who appears in a variety of forms from Scandinavia to India (although in the Indian version the cat becomes a jackal). Published in an Italian collection of stories and fables, the story was translated into French in 1585 and thence, through the version of *Le Maître Chat ou Le Chat Botté*, which was included by Charles Perrault in his *Contes des Fées* in 1696, it found its way to British nurseries.

It is not a moral tale, for it tells how a young man, with no effort on his part at all beyond a display of good manners and good looks, was helped by the lies and cunning of his opportunist cat to gain a magnificent castle and a princess as his bride. The young man, however, was a youngest son, deprived of any inheritance except the cat, so perhaps the story was intended to give some encouragement to all those younger sons whom the rules of primogeniture left bereft of opportunity. As for the boots, they would not have been much use to a real cat but they should perhaps be seen as some sort of class symbol in an age when so many would have had no proper footwear.

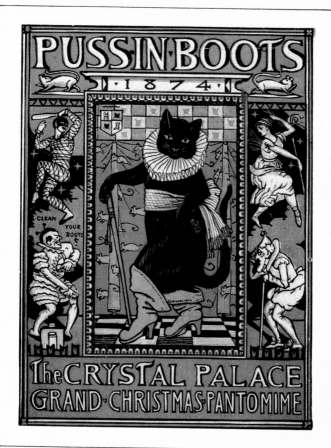

PUSS IN BOOTS
· 1 8 7 4 ·

The CRYSTAL PALACE
GRAND · CHRISTMAS · PANTOMIME

Turn Again Whittington

The most famous English story of a *matagot* cat, bringing fame and fortune to his master is that of Richard Whittington, Lord Mayor of London, three times in succession, in the fifteenth century.

The legend describes how, as a poor boy, Richard walked all the way from his home in Gloucestershire to London where, he had heard, the streets were 'paved with gold'. Unfortunately all Richard could find was a scullion's job and a place to sleep plagued with rats. He found a cat to keep down the rats but then turned his back on London and set off with this cat until on Highgate Hill he heard the bells of London telling him to turn back (a stone stands there to mark the place today).

His fellow-servants invested in one of their master's trading voyages, but all Dick had to venture was his cat, whom he sent away to see the world and keep the rats down on the ship. The palace of the potentate of the Spice Islands was plagued with rats and the cat destroyed them all, earning his master a fine reward which formed the basis of his fortune. Financial success followed and marriage to his master's daughter.

Sadly the 'cat' in the story was not a feline but probably an *achat* (purchase) or a cat boat, a single-masted vessel which plied between Newcastle and London carrying coal and timber, so simple trade was a more likely path to fortune than rodent control.

LONDON 11 MILES

31

Two-tailed Devils

These cats with two tails would be immediately recognized as devil cats in Japan, and the figure behind them is a witch that, if you note the paw, is clearly turning into a cat herself. It is a scene from a *Kabuki* play telling the story of the cruel witch cat of Okabe on the Tokaido Road.

Japanese folklore includes many stories of witch cats and vampire cats, such as the one of the cat that killed a prince's favourite concubine and then took her form until it was discovered lapping oil from a lantern at night when its head was finally recognized as that of a cat – as Kuniyoshi shows in this version of the Okabe story.

Not all tales are of bad cats. One tells of the *Maneki-neko*, the beckoning cat which used to encourage passers-by to leave the main road and visit the lowly temple where she guarded the manuscripts from mice. So many visitors did she attract that now her temple is a very rich one. Figures of the *Maneki-neko*, its paw raised in a beckoning gesture, are often carried as lucky talismans or kept in the house to bring good luck. They can often be seen in shop doorways in Japan where the proprietors hope that they will entice customers inside.

Real Japanese cats do not have two tails but many of them do have very short tails which curl and look even smaller. The western breed developed from them, known as the Japanese bobtail, is said to shed less hair than other breeds. Its body conformation and its head shape differ from other types of cat.

33

Cat and Bird

> These vilanous false cattes
> Were made for mise and rattes,
> And not for birdes smale . .

Thus wrote the fifteen-century poet John Skelton in his long lament on the death of a pet sparrow at the jaws of

> Gib our cat savage
> That in a furious rage
> Caught Phillip by the head,
> And slew him there stark dead.

Birds, like rodents, are a feline's natural prey and it is naive to expect a cat to overcome its primeval instincts. But sometimes a bird will turn the tables. The nineteenth-century zoologist George Romanes recorded an instance of a parrot which was pestered by a cat. It retaliated by calling the cat into the kitchen where it succeeded, with great accuracy, in dropping a basin of milk on top of the cat, which retreated, vanquished.

In catching rodents, cats pause before the final pounce, a habit they must suppress if they are to catch a bird before it flies away. A cat will sit on a window-sill avidly watching the birds outside, often making an excited, machine-gun-like chatter at the quarry out of reach but, despite their urge to do so, many cats lack the skill to catch birds.

The White Cat

Unlike the black cat, the white cat was considered unlucky in Britain but elsewhere the opposite was often true. A white cat features in an ancient Egyptian story and is the heroine of a fairy-tale written by the Comtesse d'Aulnoy in 1682, from which she found her way into Tchaikovsky's ballet, *The Sleeping Beauty*.

A pair of short-haired white cats imported into Britain from Japan at the end of the last century were highly thought of as symbols of purity.

White is not a common colour in the wild; in most of the cats' habitats it would make them more noticeable to their prey. It has another disadvantage too, for when coupled with blue eyes it is almost invariably linked with deafness – a problem that occurs in all cat types. Fortunately, white cats with different- or odd-coloured eyes, or with a patch of another colour in the fur, are not affected. Kittens born with a small dark patch of fur avoid hearing loss, although as they grow up, the dark fur may disappear.

White cats are also more likely to have extra toes. Polydactylism is not harmful and someone has coined the phrase 'super-scratchers' for such cats.

White patching on cats is more frequent in Asia than in Europe. Researchers found that three times as many Singaporean than London cats had more than two-thirds of their coat white and that Calcutta cats were also heavily white. Perhaps there is natural selection for white in the tropics to reflect the sunshine.

The White Cat

Find the Master

Henry Wriothesley, the 3rd Earl of Southampton, a patron of William Shakespeare, supported the Earl of Essex's abortive attempt at rebellion. His life was spared, but he was imprisoned in the Tower of London where his portrait – with his cat next to him – was painted in 1602 or 1603. According to Thomas Pennant, writing in the late eighteenth century, the cat was the Earl's favourite pet. Southampton's London house was in Holborn and the story goes that the cat made its own way to the Tower, climbed across the roof and searched until he found the chimney of the apartment where the earl was lodged and then climbed down to join its master.

If that seems quite a feat, it is nothing compared with many other stories of cats seeking out their owners in quite unknown territory after they have been left behind. One cat called Sugar evaded his owners when they set off from California for a new home in Oklahoma. Fourteen months later, he turned up at their new home. Apart from appearance and behaviour a bone deformity confirmed that this really was their cat. One of the most remarkable instances of this kind involved a cat belonging to a New York vet which he left behind when taking up a new post on the West Coast in California. Five months later, the cat had traced his master in California, making a journey of at least 2300 miles to reach him.

The Chairman

Many photographers and artists in the mid-nineteenth century showed little real respect for cats when they dressed them up in doll's or human's clothes and made them appear more human than feline. Louis Wain, known as 'the man who drew cats', went further than this. Both he and his cats lived in Catland, in an Edwardian era reflecting confidence and optimism. Wain was born in 1860 and died, certified insane, in 1939. He managed to write a great deal as well as paint, contributing to papers, to the National Cat Club publications and he produced countless books and annuals on cats. Reproductions of his works were printed in their thousands and today his work is avidly collected.

His madness developed slowly and might initially have been considered mere eccentricity but was in fact the onset of severe schizophrenia. Some of his paintings, done in his seventies in the asylum to which he was confined, reflect his illness, the shapes of the cats disappearing into dazzling patterns of curious beauty.

An appropriate epitaph, written in fact two years before his death, appeared in *Everybody's Weekly*, 'He laughed at cats – until they robbed him of wealth, health and reason'.

Lucky Tortoishell

Owning a tortoiseshell cat will bring good luck according to both Japanese and American folklore. Japanese sailors believed that if a tortoiseshell cat was sent up a mast it could drive storm demons away.

One American cat seems to have shown a very suitable spirit. President Theodore Roosevelt's pet Slippers was always in attendance at White House dinners and state occasions during his term of office, but his presence was undoubtably due to his taste for good food rather than any great patriotic sense.

There have been many other statesmen fond of cats. Abraham Lincoln rescued and adopted three orphaned cats he found on a visit to General Grant's camp; Winston Churchill had a ginger tom which would join him at War Cabinet meetings; French Premier Leon Blum kept a Siamese at the Elysée Palace and Georges Clemenceau a Blue Persian and, although Napoleon Bonaparte was said to be terrified of cats, Lenin was very fond of them.

William Langland, a fourteenth-century English poet, borrowed a medieval fable and had a cat, representing the nobility, in the person of John of Gaunt who played with the English Commons, play with mice: a council of mice and rats bought a bell and hung it on a collar – but none dared attach it to the cat. This satire on contemporary society reflects the feelings that helped to spark off the Peasants' Revolt which was ruthlessly suppressed.

Nine Lives

Cats seem to take fantastic risks escaping from dangerous situations. Whether climbing out on a fragile branch, leaping across a roof-top or spitting insults at a dog, they are rarely actually at risk. For every cat that has to be rescued from a tree by the fire brigade, there are probably a dozen more that wonder what all the fuss is for and make their own way back to safety.

The cat's nine lives owe less to providence than to its reactions and the skill with which it can use its finely adjusted body. Its skeleton is unexceptional, but its head can turn much further and it is everywhere more flexible. It has a prodigious sense of smell; its hearing is acute over a much wider range than man's and it has a well-developed sense of touch. It cannot see in the dark although it sees well in light conditions ranging from bright sunshine to the very dim in which man's eyes would register no light at all. Some specialization, presumably that of the inner ear, which is not yet understood, gives it an amazing sense of balance. While many dogs and people are travel-sick, a healthy cat is immune to the discomfort of a rocking boat or moving car. This must be linked with a cat's ability to right itself when falling, although tests with deaf animals have shown that sight also plays a part in this process. These abilities, the powerful spring given by its back legs and a skill at judging distances, save it in situations which would bring disaster to many other animals.

A Feast in Fairyland

Now, here they are waiting, all sitting in state,
See the snowy white cloth, and each shiny white plate,
    And every one eager and anxious to know
    What's coming for dinner – the servants are slow!
There's only at present a big pastry pie;
Is it good as it looks? They are longing to try.
    They're all of them needing a glass and a fork,
    And while they are waiting a few of them talk.
There's a Giant – before him is Hop-o'-my-Thumb.
And Robinson Crusoe, he also has come.
    There's sweet-tempered Beauty beside her dear Beast.
    Aladdin has brought his old lamp to the feast,
He's telling its marvels to Little Bo-Peep.
Who does not look happy, she longs for her sheep;
    She fears they will wander again far away,
    Awhile she is feasting so finely to day;
Boy Blue is conversing with Red Riding Hood
About the adventures she had in the wood;
    Next – holding the key – is bad Bluebeard's last wife;
    With her shoe, Cinderella – just look at her knife!
'Tis a wonderful party; no greatest no least,
Three cheers for our friends at this Fairyland Feast.

G.C.F.

A FEAST IN FAIRYLAND

Louis Wain

Sources and Acknowledgements

5. Tomb painting, Egyptian, 18th Dynasty (British Museum)
7. Tomb painting, Egyptian, 18th Dynasty (British Museum)
9. Roman mosaic, Pompeii, first century BC (Mansell Collection)
11. Bestiary, thirteenth century (British Library)
13. Engraving, nineteenth century
15. *The Country Mouse and the Town Mouse* by Kay Nielsen from *Red Magic*, 1930 (Private Collection)
17. Engraving by Randolph Caldecott for *The House that Jack Built*, 1875
19. *Sam, the All-American Cat* by Robert McAulay, 1978 (Private Collection)
21. Painting by Stephen Aris (Portal Gallery)
23. Painting by Murata Kokoku, 1866 (Erika Bruce Collection)
25. Wood-block print by Kuniyoshi (1798-1861)
27. Lithography by Jacques Nam from Colette, *Chats*, 1930 (Private Collection)
29. Pantomime poster, Crystal Palace (Private Collection)
31. Pantomime poster, Garrick Theatre
33. Wood-block print by Yoshifuji (1828-1887) (Private Collection)
35. Indian painting, Kanagra school , *c*.1810 (Victoria and Albert Museum)
37. Drawn by E. MacKinstry for *The White Cat and Other Fairy Tales* by Mme la Comtesse d'Aulnoy, 1928 edition
39. Painting attributed to John de Critz (By courtesy of Duke of Buccleuch KT, Boughton House, Kettering, England)
41. Painting by Louis Wain
43. Engraving, nineteenth century (Private Collection)
45. Painting by Sylvia Emmons (Courtesy of the artist)
47. Jigsaw by Louis Wain published by Raphael Tuck and Sons Ltd, 1909
Title page: watercolour by Carole Thompson
The publishers would like to thank Ellery Wood for her help in producing this book